Rookie
Read-About®
Health

DISCARD

I Lost a Tooth

by **Lisa M. Herrington**

Content Consultant
Jeffrey Pivor, D.D.S.

Reading Consultant
Jeanne M. Clidas, Ph.D.
Reading Specialist

Children's Press®
An Imprint of Scholastic Inc.
New York Toronto London Auckland Sydney
Mexico City New Delhi Hong Kong
Danbury, Connecticut

Library of Congress Cataloging-in-Publication Data
Herrington, Lisa M.
 I lost a tooth/by Lisa M. Herrington.
     pages cm. — (Rookie read-about health)
Summary: "Introduces the reader to how baby teeth are lost, what to do when it
happens, as well as the different kinds of teeth in the human mouth"— Provided by
publisher.
Audience: Ages 3-6
Includes bibliographical references and index.
 ISBN 978-0-531-21013-0 (library binding: alk. paper) — ISBN 978-0-531-21070-3
(pbk.: alk. paper)
1. Deciduous teeth—Juvenile literature. 2. Teeth—Juvenile literature. 3. Tooth loss—
Juvenile literature. I. Title. II. Series: Rookie read-about health.

 QP88.6.H47 2015
 612.3'11—dc23   .   2014035901

Produced by Spooky Cheetah Press
Design by Keith Plechaty

© 2015 by Scholastic Inc.

1 2 3 4 5 6 7 8 9 10 R 24 23 22 21 20 19 18 17 16 15

Photographs: Alamy Images: 12, 31 center bottom (Scott Camazine), 20
(wonderlandstock); Getty Images/Peter Dazeley: cover; iStockphoto: 29 bottom
right (cveltri), 31 bottom (drbimages), 3 top left (rimglow), 4 (vgajic), 29 bottom
left (Yarinca); Media Bakery: 8, 31 top (Hero), 11 (Streetfly Stock); Science Source/
Ken Cavanagh: 23; Shutterstock, Inc.: 31 center top (Lighthunter), 3 bottom (Tyler
Olson), 7 (Stock Connection); Thinkstock: 29 top right (Arvind Balaraman), 19
(BananaStock), 27 (Darrin Henry), 24 (Jodi Jacobson), 28 (Marcel Braendli), 30
(VYCHEGZHANINA), 16, 29 top left (Wavebreakmedia Ltd), 3 top right (Zheka-Boss).

Illustration by Jeffrey Chandler/Art Gecko Studios!

Table of Contents

Wiggly and Wobbly

Wiggle, wiggle, wiggle. Your tiny tooth is loose. It finally falls out. You lost a tooth!

Smile! There is a hole where your tooth was. A new tooth will grow in its place. Losing teeth is part of growing up.

Your teeth let you talk, eat, and smile.

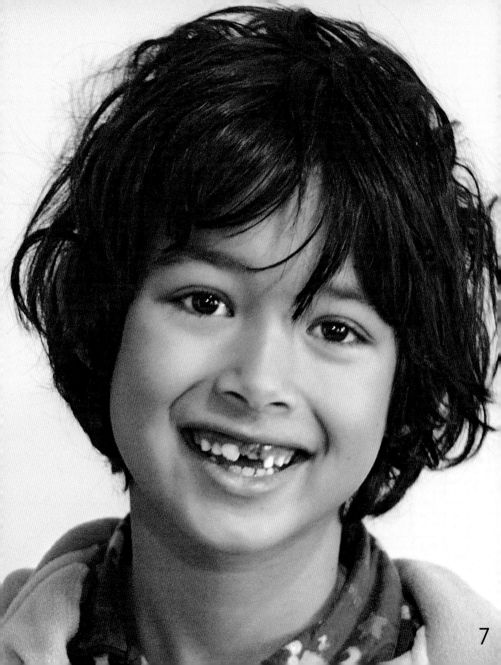

On the Way Out

Kids have 20 **baby teeth.**
They start to lose them around
ages five and six.

FAST FACT!

Most kids grow their full set
of baby teeth by age three.

Teeth often fall out in the order they first grew in. So the two bottom middle teeth usually fall out first. The top two are next.

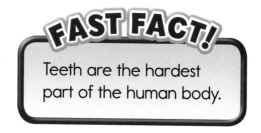

FAST FACT!

Teeth are the hardest part of the human body.

permanent
teeth

New teeth under your **gums** push out baby teeth. The new teeth are called **permanent teeth**.

Most kids finish losing their baby teeth around age 12 or 13. Besides the baby teeth that are replaced, more permanent teeth grow in the back of the mouth. Adults have a total of 32 teeth.

When permanent teeth come in, they look different from baby teeth.

Terrific Teeth

Your teeth are different shapes. That is because they do different jobs. The first baby teeth you lose are usually incisors. They are sharp and are used to cut food. The other front teeth are canines. These pointy teeth tear food. Molars are the back teeth. They crush and grind food.

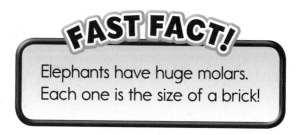

FAST FACT!

Elephants have huge molars. Each one is the size of a brick!

Types of Teeth

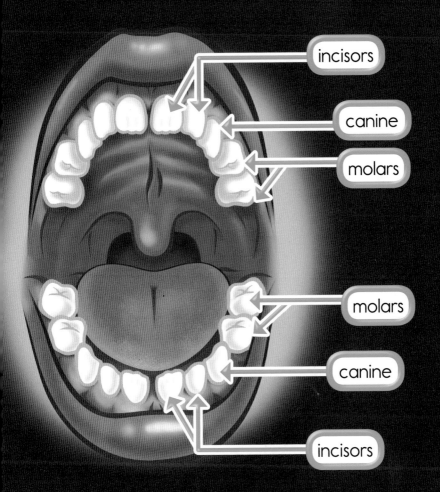

incisors

canine

molars

molars

canine

incisors

It is important to keep your baby teeth and permanent teeth healthy. Brush twice a day. You should also floss once a day. Flossing removes germs and food that may be caught between teeth.

Brush in the morning and at night.

Eating right builds strong teeth. Eating too many sugary foods can cause **cavities**. Germs in your mouth feed on sugar. The germs make acid that attack teeth. The acid can lead to cavities.

FAST FACT!

Visit the dentist twice a year. A dentist cleans teeth and checks for cavities.

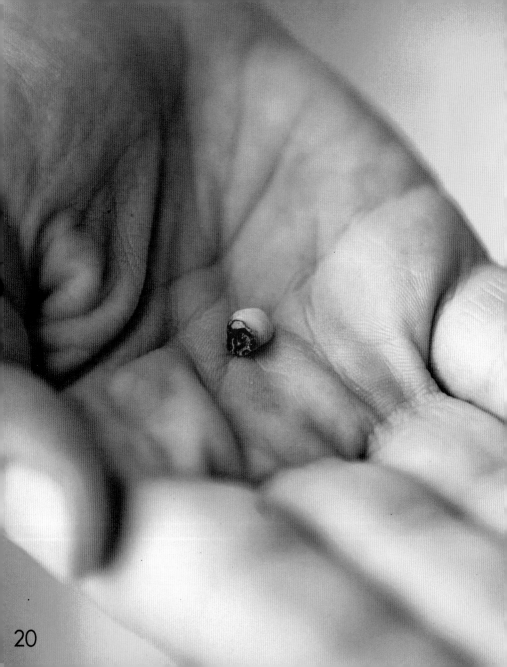

Your Changing Smile

You may not know what to expect when you lose a tooth. Chances are you will not feel a thing. You may bleed a little. The bleeding will stop quickly, though.

A loose tooth may feel funny. Try to let it come out on its own. A loose tooth may fall out when you eat. Do not pull a tooth before it is ready.

FAST FACT!

After a baby tooth falls out, a new tooth can take up to a few weeks to appear.

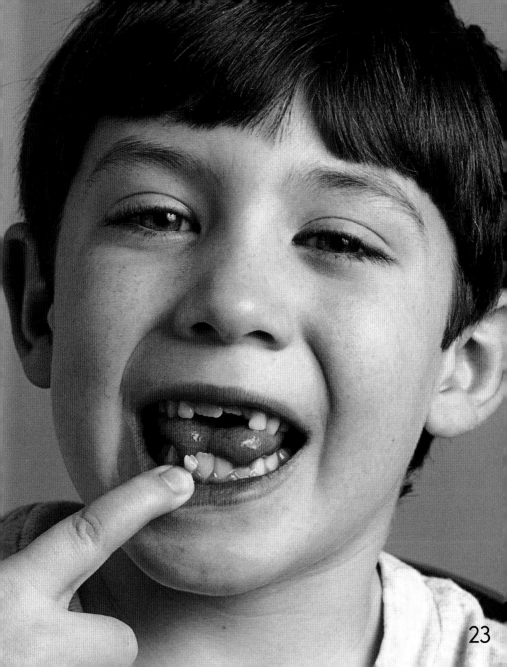

If the tooth is ready to come out, it is okay to gently wiggle it. You can use your tongue or a clean finger. Check with your dentist if a loose tooth is not coming out.

As you get bigger, your teeth change. They are growing with you!

Healthy teeth help make your smile beautiful.

Let's explore your teeth!

1. Count your teeth. How many do you have? How many are baby teeth? How many are permanent teeth? Do you have any missing teeth?

2. Use your tongue or a clean finger to feel along the edges of your four front teeth. Do all the teeth feel the same or are some different? How are they different?

A Healthy Smile

Look at the photos below. Which one is *not* a good way to care for your teeth?

1.

2.

3.

4.

Answer: 2. Sweets are special treats. Sugary foods are not good for your teeth. Brushing, flossing, and visiting the dentist all help with a healthy smile.

Strange but True!

Long ago, people used hair from pigs and horses to clean their teeth. They attached the hairs to sticks. Early toothpastes were made from crushed rocks and shells. This harsh toothpaste actually caused damage by scraping off parts of the teeth!

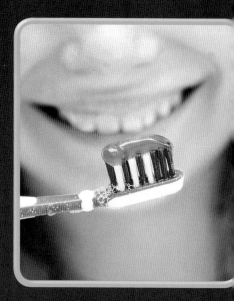

Just for Fun

Q: What has teeth but no mouth?

A: A comb!

Q: What keeps teeth from falling out?

A: Toothpaste!

Glossary

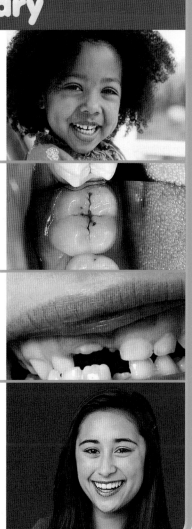

baby teeth (BAY-bee TEETH): first set of 20 teeth that fall out

cavities (KAV-uh-teez): rotted parts of teeth

gums (GUHMZ): soft pink lining around the teeth

permanent teeth (PUR-muh-nuhnt TEETH): 32 adult teeth that replace baby teeth

Index

Facts for Now

Visit this Scholastic Web site for more information on teeth:
www.factsfornow.scholastic.com
Enter the keyword **Teeth**

About the Author

Lisa M. Herrington is the author of many books and articles for kids. She lives in Trumbull, Connecticut, with her husband, Ryan, and daughter, Caroline. As a child, Lisa got excited whenever she had a loose tooth!